HOW TO ANALYZE PEOPLE

UNCOVER SHERLOCK HOLMES' SECRETS TO ANALYZE ANYONE ON THE SPOT. ACCOMPAGNIED BY DIY SOCIAL-MASTERY EXPERIMENTS

PATRICK LIGHTMAN

How to Analyze People like Sherlock

Uncover Sherlock Holmes' Secrets to Analyze Anyone on the Spot.

Accompanied by DIY social-mastery experiments.

By Patrick Lightman

How to Analyze People like Sherlock Holmes

Uncover Sherlock Holmes' Secrets to Analyze Anyone on the Spot. Accompanied by DIY social-mastery experiments.

Copyright © 2019 by Patrick Lightman

Table of Contents

Introduction

The year was 1886. Arthur Conan Doyle was running a struggling surgery clinic in Portsmouth, but had other preoccupations in mind. He wanted to write, and so write he did.

Deeply inspired by his mentor, Dr. Joseph Bell who could provide a near accurate - or in some cases - even a perfect diagnosis upon looking at a patient, Conan Doyle was fueled with imagination and creativity in the 3 weeks that it took to write his first ever Sherlock Holmes novel - *A Study in Scarlet*.

Following his incessant writing and sleepless nights, the proud doctor approached a handful of publishers, all of which turned their backs on his book and closed their doors. It wasn't until he was able to sell his book to the *Beeton's Christmas Annual* that his book received *some* publicity.

The *Beeton's Christmas Annual* at the time contained *A Study in Scarlet,* and two original drawing room plays, all buried together in a sea of advertisements. The year was 1887, and the paperback magazine sold out before Christmas at the cost of 1 shilling per copy.

While the rapid sales would have you assume that Conan Doyle probably met success shortly after that year's Christmas, he didn't. The physician-turned-author was quoted saying that "the book had no particular success at the time", a truth that was proven by the general lack of interest in both Arthur and his eccentric detective character.

When he sold *A Study in Scarlet* to Beeton's, he was offered no more than £25 for the copyright. Initially, the doctor tried to argue and bargain. But due to the lack of offers and interest in his book, he had no choice but to agree to the deal.

Sad as it may seem, the now iconic author earned nothing more than that initial £25 on his first ever Holmes masterpiece which today sells roughly $20 a copy and is often considered a vintage classic. Even as the initial novel gained popularity as Sherlock Holmes became more prominent throughout the years, Conan Doyle saw no royalties since he sold the copyright entirely.

At the time, it seems people weren't as interested in the intellectual exploits of Sherlock Holmes, and perhaps his unconventional behavior and investigative work flew over their heads.

But as time went on, more and more people started to pick up on Sherlock's astounding detective prowess, turning both Conan Doyle and his character into a success after 1890 when the second installment of the series was published.

Although it didn't quite receive the acclaim that Conan Doyle had hoped, details in *A Study in Scarlet* established the kind of character Sherlock was and the skills he possessed that would make him iconic in pop culture 130 years down the line.

His disdain for social mores, his remarkable fastidiousness, his habit of selecting only interesting cases, and his exemplary capacity to accurately profile any person at a glance all made him the most filmed fictional human character since the advent of cinematic film. This, and of course, one of the most popular idols for people who want to make use of their mind in the most efficient ways possible.

Flashing back to *A Study in Scarlet* when Holmes first meets Watson, we're given a glimpse as to how impressive the super sleuth actually is when it comes to deciphering people at a glance. With no more than one look, Sherlock tells his new acquaintance that he presumed the doctor had come from Afghanistan after serving in the war.

Was he correct? Absolutely. Did anyone tell him? Absolutely not. So how exactly did he come to infer such specific information? It all lies in his impeccable capacity to *analyze anyone on the spot.*

While very few of us are considered to be super sleuths in this modern day and age, there are countless benefits to learning *how* to read people. Giving us the capability to call the right shots, make the right move, and avoid confrontation all before it happens, learning to analyze people upon meeting them can improve your relationship and help you become far more efficient at social interactions.

So, if you're tired of bickering over misunderstandings with friends and family, if you're sick of hearing your boss tell you that you've misinterpreted his instructions yet again, if you're hoping to make new friends, keep old ones, and experience a stress-free social life, then the answer might be right here.

Find out how you can turn Sherlock Holmes' master investigator capabilities into real-life skills that you can use in any social situation.

Chapter 1 - Inside the Mind of Sherlock Holmes

"And these other people?"

"They are mostly sent on by private inquiry agencies. They are all people who are in trouble about something, and want a little enlightening. I listen to their story, they listen to my comments, and then I pocket my fee."

"But do you mean to say," I said, "that without leaving your room you can unravel some knot which other men can make nothing of, although they have seen every detail for themselves?"

"Quite so. I have a kind of intuition that way."

- Dialogue between Sherlock Holmes and John Watson, A Study in Scarlet

What made Sherlock such a success at his trade? Why did established police officers and authorities come to him for guidance and assistance? Why was he the go-to name in London for anyone and everyone looking for answers - regardless of whether or not he was familiar with their particular situation?

In A Study in Scarlet, Sherlock tells Watson a little more about himself and his skill, and the doctor finds himself intrigued by the super sleuth's popularity as an investigator, leading him to believe that perhaps, the man's strange ethic did in fact hold some value.

Throughout the Sherlock Holmes series, we read about the master detective constantly surprising the good doctor with conclusions and inferences that seem to have come from nothing more than scant, often seemingly irrelevant evidence. This is what makes him popular, and this is what makes him a reliable professional in his respective field.

One other skill that came hand in hand with Sherlock's impeccable detective capabilities was his knack for deciphering people at a mere glance. He showcased this skill early on in the first novel, where he tells Watson - upon meeting for the first time - that he perceived the doctor had served in Afghanistan.

Having just met and not knowing much about each other aside from their names and their trade, Watson was baffled at how Holmes knew something so specific. For a while, the doctor was convinced that someone had told him of Watson's exploits serving in the Anglo-Afghan war.

Later on in the book, Sherlock explains that no one had told him anything. Instead, he simply took what he was based on the doctor's appearances and put the pieces together from there. Unnaturally dark skin, an injured arm, and a tired face to go with his stiff army doctor demeanor. Where else would the man have been other than Afghanistan, Sherlock surmised.

These days, there are very few people who can decode others at a glance the same way Holmes did. In fact, with so many distractions, charades, styles, personalities, cultures, and influences working within and around us, it has become increasingly difficult to understand people at a glance.

But a first-time meet isn't the only time when these influences might work against us. Even in well-established relationships, misunderstandings occur because we *can't* completely grasp how others around us think, act, and behave. So we end up clashing with them, battling it out because we have our own perspectives.

If we could adapt Sherlock's skill for interpreting others and deciphering people at a glance, then we might be able to mitigate misunderstandings, miscommunication, and arguments across our social interactions.

So how do we do it? First let's take a look into the Sherlock Holmes method for socialization.

Clarity

One of the principles that Sherlock fervently believes in is the importance of silence when dealing with any situation. During his investigative work, he would often refrain from speaking, and would often be seen with his eyes closed and his fingers pressed against each other as if deep in thought. Why did he do this?

Sherlock believed that clarity of mind was an important facet of properly understanding a situation - or in other cases, people. Having a clutter-free mind that's prepared to take information without any interference from your own thoughts, ideas, and prejudices reduces noise and prevents misinterpretation.

Detachment

How can detachment help when it comes to social interactions? Shouldn't we be eager, willing, and excited to communicate, socialize, and participate in conversation and interaction if we want to properly understand the people around us? If that were the case, then perhaps Sherlock Holmes would have been far less talented at deciphering people at a glance.

Although it seems counterintuitive, the best

way to actually understand a person is by detaching yourself from the interaction. This has something to do with clarity, and prevents your mind from labeling certain factors and interpreting them how you might be inclined to.

Consider this: you're a well-educated young professional and you've been looking for business partners to help you build and fund a small enterprise that you've been planning for a while. As you're having lunch one day, a man in a suit, looking polished and well-off, walks into the restaurant.

He sits at the table across from yours and orders nothing more than the most expensive wine on the restaurant's menu. He then pulls out his smartphone and calls up who you assume is his business partner. They're talking numbers.

With your limited knowledge of corporate talk, you figure that this man is minted and that he has funds to spare. In fact, it sounds like he might be looking to invest in a business idea just like yours.

Do you approach him? If you would, what would you say and how would you say it?

Now, before we dissect that scenario, consider this second situation. You've walked out of the restaurant after having your lunch and a teenager approaches you. You scan his appearance quickly and see that he's wearing raggedy old clothes, and it seems as though it's been a while since the last time he took a bath given the stench that's coming off of him.

He wants to talk to you about a monetary donation that he wants to use for his education. But as he talks, you notice what seem to be needle marks covering his forearm.

What do you do? Do you let him finish talking, and how do you deal with this particular person?

Most of those who read the first encounter would say that they'd put their best foot forward. This person was *exactly* the kind of funder and business mentor that you need, so it would be highly beneficial for you to be able to get on his good side. In the second situation however, you might not have been too kind. Some might say that they would have turned the teenager away because he was probably lying to fund an addiction.

But, did you notice something about these typical reactions? For the most part, we as humans have a tendency to react based on our *emotions*. How will this person benefit me? Is this someone I want to associate myself with? What will I gain out of engaging with this person?

Learning to detach the self from the situation and regarding a person without bias helps prevent you from acting in a way that leans towards your own egocentric tendencies. That's often how arguments and misunderstandings happen in the first place - because most of us are wired to look at a person and think, *how will this interaction benefit me?*

In some cases, attachment also occurs when it comes to the way we perceive ourselves. Some people feel that they should interact only with those that they feel fall within similar socioeconomic or cultural barriers. Anyone who *seems* to fall outside of those limits might be approached with caution, or not at all.

Observation

Once you're free from mental clutter and persona bias, it then becomes easier to observe in detail. Sherlock showcased his keen eye for observation multiple times throughout the series, which actually contributed greatly to his success and popularity.

For instance, in *The Hound of the Baskervilles*, he revealed his thought process at the end of the novel, including the reason why one of Sr. Henry's boots had gone missing. He claimed that the first boot used in the investigation didn't work because the hounds couldn't get a scent off of it since it was brand new. This was also the reason why the other boots had gone missing as an attempt to hide evidence.

To anyone investigating the same case, the newness of the boot might not have been an object of interest. But for Sherlock, it became the turning point that ultimately led to the arrest.

Having this kind of keen eye for observation doesn't only help reveal truths about a situation, but may also shed light on how you should approach a new acquaintance. Taking notes on how a person is dressed, how they approach you, their body language, facial expressions, tone of voice, and virtually every aspect of their being before, during, and after an interaction can help you better understand how to deal with them.

Demeanor

There's no question that social interaction is just a series of reactions between people - even before they've actually engaged. Eye contact, posture, facial expressions - we all take these things into account without knowing it, and then fashion our approach and reactions based on what the other person is feeding us.

While previous discussions in this guide should have already taught you *not* to let someone else's demeanor dictate your reactions, it's equally important to make sure *you're* not doing anything to inhibit a person from being guarded. What does that mean?

Answer this question: Do you think a stranger would like to approach you or talk to you if you had your arms crossed over your chest, and your brows furrowed down the middle of your forehead? Probably not. If they did decide to talk to you, they might feel intimidated, or they might try to act with slight hostility and aggression to show you that your intimidation tactics don't work.

In any case, having the wrong demeanor could interfere with a person's real behavior, causing them to act a certain way as a response to your aura. This could interfere with your observations, and lead you to call the wrong shots later on.

Sherlock *knew* that his physical behavior could cause differences in the way the people around him would act, so he devised a way to make sure that his demeanor wouldn't get in the way of his efforts to collect evidence. That was, he would make sure that he would adopt an aura of neutrality, and depending on the case, he would lean slightly towards a slight irritability or slight concern.

Why? A neutral, open demeanor made people around him feel that they weren't being judged, so they didn't feel the need to act in a way that deflects his judgment. If you've read any of the Sherlock Holmes novels, you'll find that that's how he would often manage to get face to face with a perpetrator, allowing them to feel comfortable and unjudged in his presence, and encouraging them to speak and share their alibis as Holmes absorbed the information and pieced together his case.

In some cases, Holmes would be neutral yet mildly irritable, especially when dealing with people he only needed to deliver facts. Inspector Lestrade, for example, was a detective inspector who often asked Sherlock for his assistance whenever he would reach a dead end. Holmes had no fondness nor appreciation for Lestrade, and only really accepted his requests as he needed money.

So in many of their interactions, you'll find that Sherlock would often showcase slight irritability that made Lestrade provide him all the information he needed minus unnecessary pleasantries. In this instance, his demeanor would definitely still be useful, allowing him to get all the details of the case and making no room for interactions that might eat up time for no reason.

In certain cases, you might also find Sherlock acting with slight concern. This was often what he would do when dealing with private individuals that would seek him for assistance on the disappearance or death of a loved one. Over time, it would also be the way he would approach Watson who became a very close friend of his as the series progressed.

Chapter 2 - Understand Yourself First

"I'm not a psychopath. I'm a high functioning sociopath. Do your research."

\- Sherlock Holmes, TV Series

If there's anything that Sherlock was an expert at, it was *knowing himself.* The super sleuth understood his own mind, and that made it easy for him to control himself, his thoughts, and his actions. Having full jurisdiction over his own cognition allowed the master investigator to make calculated decisions and quick however accurate calculations of *who people were* - all done in lightning speed.

Being able to *know yourself* is an essential step in the entire process of learning about others. Knowing your own personality type, decoding your tendencies when faced with social interactions, and learning how to alter your own demeanor to encourage outsiders to approach, talk, and act unguarded are important facets of becoming an expert at decoding those around you.

What's Your Social Personality Type?

First of all, it's important to know what your social personality type is. While there are a variety of tests that you can take online to give you a *label* to go with your usual socialization trends, there is no better way to truly grasp how you are as a social creature than by *metacognition.*

It takes a lot of mindfulness to be able to *think* about the way you *think*, especially during social interaction. But in doing so, you can unlock some realities that might not have seemed apparent at the start. To begin the process, try asking yourself these questions:

1. When was the last time I argued with

someone? What were the sequence of events that led to the rift? Did I show any behaviors that might have aggravated the situation? How could I have improved the outcomes of our interaction?

2. Who do I consider my closest or best friend? How did I meet this person? What might this individual appreciate about the way I interact with him or her?

3. When faced with a stranger, what is my initial reaction? How do I choose to present myself? Am I talkative and overbearing, taking control of the conversation from the start? Or do I prefer to let the stranger lead?

4. Are there times when I feel compelled to engage in interaction, or to completely avoid it? When does this happen and why do I sometimes feel that way?

Now that you know the answers to these questions, you might already have some sort of understanding of your socialization trend. Some might have found themselves to be particularly friendly even with strangers, others might be more standoffish or intimidating. Whatever the case, it's highly probable that your social personality *isn't the ideal* one for decoding strangers.

The purpose of this exercise wasn't exactly to help you put a name on your socialization trend, but rather to teach you *how to ask yourself the right questions* in order to audit your own personality. Knowing how to think about and process the way you engage with others can shed light on errors in your approach and provide you feedback that you can use to become more efficient in future encounters.

The next time you find yourself in a social interaction gone-wrong, take a moment to trace back your steps. What happened? Where did the conversation turn sour? And what can you do now to try to neutralize the situation and avoid confrontation?

Asking yourself these questions even in the middle of an argument should help you reflect on your behavior at that given moment. It also helps to reflect on previous confrontations you might have had. Taking the time to understand how things might have gone wrong in the past will help you avoid the same mistakes in the future. This way, you can have a more polished approach and a broader idea as to the proper behavior during your next social interactions.

Finally, you might also want to consider whether there have been instances when you experienced the same issues. Patterns in your behavior could cause the same problems to arise, even if you're dealing with different people.

Taking a look back at previous encounters and trying to find trends can show you where you're most likely to fail during a social interaction. Some people might find that the problem lies in tactlessness, some find that the issue stems from their fixation on certain topics that a majority of individuals might find touchy or insulting.

Most of the time, these trends can be discovered with metacognition alone. However, there are some people who might need to experience confrontation once more to be able to accurately pinpoint where the problem exists. In this case, try to be mindful of what triggered the response during your interaction and make a mental note of the events as they occurred. This should make it easier to relieve the trend and adopt a healthier manner of interaction.

The Right Way to Behave

Imagine walking into a therapist's clinic for the first time. You've been invited to visit so that you can talk about childhood traumas, personal fears, problems, and other issues that might be eating up a part of your mental bandwidth. Needless to say, these are very personal, private concerns that you might not want to share, even with the closest people in your life.

So how do you think the therapist should act if she wants to get the most honest information out of your meeting? If she had her arms crossed over her chest, if she chuckled when you shared particularly touchy information, if she winced at some of your stories, would you feel comfortable proceeding?

What if she were *too* accommodating? Asking a

lot of questions? Overly reactive and empathizing with everything you said? Would she seem suspicious or pretentious? Would you feel comfortable continuing the session?

If there's anyone in present day that we can take cues from, it's therapists and counselors. Although their methods aren't entirely Holmesian, they do come pretty close. Their neutrality, their capability to ask the right questions at the right time, and their controlled reactions encourage people to share more truth without pretenses.

Given that, we can take away these basic aspects of the proper way to confront social interaction:

1. **Non-confrontational** - Have you ever noticed how a therapist might continue to sit comfortably even when their client stands up, starts pacing, and acts agitated? It's a basic part of their profession to remain calm even in the face of an unsettled client.

Adapting a confrontational or aggressive demeanor can trigger one of two responses in your conversational partner and they look a lot like fight or flight. Those who have more confidence or who feel that they might have the opportunity to take the upper hand would match your aggression. Those who feel intimidated by your confrontational behavior would probably flee the situation.

Always make sure you're not displaying any signs of aggression, irritation, or anger. This helps mitigate arguments, even as the conversation becomes heated.

2. **Genuine** - How can you be pretentious when it comes to social interaction? Easy - act like you're *too interested or invested* in what's being communicated. While it is absolutely possible to feel certain emotions especially when your conversational partner starts sharing touchy information, acting out of proportion might communicate that you're simply being theatrical.

To the person you're interacting with, the disproportionate display of emotion or reaction might be a poorly thought out strategy in order to get them to share more. The apparent lack of actual concern or care might be a turn off, which might actually cause them to hold back on how much they're willing to tell you.

How do you act *genuine* in the face of a new person? The answer isn't as complicated as it seems. Simply *be genuine*. Reacting based on how much emotion you actually feel will keep you from seeming uncaring or pretentious.

3. **Ask Only When Necessary** - If there's one thing about Sherlock that made him particularly efficient when collecting information was that he didn't interrupt anyone when they shared details with him. He would stay silent, listen intently, and keep his thoughts and ideas to himself until the person was done sharing. In many cases, Sherlock wouldn't even ask any questions at all.

Holmes firmly believed that all the information you could ever need to properly dissect a situation (or a person) could be collected based off of what you're given. Asking questions was simply an *optional* part of the process mainly because of one thing - detachment.

Sherlock didn't involve his own prejudices, biases, or thoughts when he was being given information. He took the details as they were, so he rarely ever felt the need to ask a question.

If ever he had to, it was only to clarify information that had already been given.

When dealing with a new person that you want to decode or decipher, try not to ask too many questions. Take what they say and pay attention to how they look - more often than not, you'll get everything you need out of just these two facets.

Asking questions tends to lead you down trains of thought that focus on your own egocentric tendencies, so it's often not recommended. If you find the need to ask a question, it's probably because you've allowed your thoughts or biases to interfere.

4. **Neutralize Body Language** - Later on in this guide, you'll learn just how much you can tell about a person based on body language and other non-verbal cues. These are potent markers that betray internal thoughts and feelings, allowing others to get a glimpse into a person's psyche by simply looking at how they're physically behaving.

In the same way that you can use these tools to understand the people around you, so too can others inspect your body language to learn more about you. Practicing how to neutralize your body language regardless of what might be going on in your mind can help make it a challenge for others to understand your true intentions, giving you the upper hand in any social interaction.

Generally, neutral body language starts with a neutral, relaxed posture. An open aura achieved through relaxed arms held at the side or with the hands gently clasped together can encourage another person to feel more comfortable. Leaning backward in a chair can also communicate a non-confrontational demeanor, creating a friendly atmosphere for your encounter.

Facial expressions too need to be carefully considered. Showing signs of your emotions can make a person adjust their behavior in order to mitigate any negativity they might cause you to experience. Keeping your face neutral and reacting minimally only when necessary can help maintain a natural interaction.

Honing Your Inner Holmes - DIY Experiment

Now that you've got some of the basics of behavior down, it's time to polish them with a short test. This exercise is designed to help you understand your current social behavior so that you can get a better idea of what you need to change.

1. Find a quiet outdoor space where you might find a few strangers or passers-by. Try to find a place where you can sit comfortably and people watch.

2. Choose someone in the crowd at random. Observe their appearance, demeanor, and behavior. Once you have a well-established idea of who they might be, try to answer the following questions.

   A. How would you approach this person?

   B. How do you think this person would act given your approach?

   C. Do you think you'd get along with this

person?

D. What would you talk about to get them interested in engaging with you?

3. Now, try to do some deep breathing exercises. Close your eyes, relax, and clear your mind of any thoughts that might interfere with your interactions. Take a few moments to breathe deliberately, feeling the air fill your lungs before letting out as much as you can.

4. Open your eyes and try to find the same person you observed earlier. This time, with your clear mind, try to answer the previous questions again.

5. Once you've finished answering the previous questions, try to audit your response with these guide questions.

A. How did the breathing exercises help you become more aware of your behavior?

B. Were there changes in the way you first answered the questions compared to the second attempt?

What were they?

C. What tendencies or trends did you notice about your social behavior the first time you answered the questions? For instance, did you focus on a specific set of features? Were there any biases that you might have applied to your observations?

D. Given what you've learned, how do you think you can improve your approach so that you don't impart any influence on social interactions?

Chapter 3 - How to Control Your Own Behavior

"To comprehend yourself truly, which is also to comprehend the world truly, you needn't look any farther than at what abounds with life around you – the blossoming meadow, the untrodden woodlands. Without this as mankind's overriding objective, I don't foresee an age of actual enlightenment ever arriving."

- Sherlock Holmes, A Slight Trick of the Mind

Many times, Sherlock would find himself face to face with the perpetrator of the crime he would be investigating. And while the master detective likely had a sense of certainty in knowing that the person in front of him was responsible for the crime, he would maintain his silence and tell no one, even letting the criminal leave his presence without making an attempt to apprehend him.

But why?

Holmes knew that acting out and showing any signs of suspicion would tip the perpetrator and probably cause them to act in a way that would cover up his involvement. This change in behavior could easily cause confusion, and that's not something Sherlock wanted to deal with. He knew that the less guarded the perpetrator was, the more likely they would slip up and share information that could possibly incriminate him.

In the same way, showing the wrong behavior during an interaction could cause changes in the other person's behavior. This could make them act guarded, wary, and careful, and may even cause them to enact tactics that are intended to confuse you.

While we discussed the ideal behavior in the previous chapter, the way to achieve that kind of demeanor isn't quite as obvious. How can you control yourself so that you don't end up altering the behavior of people around you?

Controlling Your Own Behavior

Watson would often describe Sherlock as being full of himself, and he would question whether the master detective even felt human emotion on the typical scale that most of us do. If anything, Holmes was an arrogant man and he *knew* for a fact that he was more intellectually capable than most others around him.

Despite that though, he was able to hold back his tendencies and keep his opinions to himself. He was exceptionally talented at maintaining neutrality and keeping his mouth shut even if he probably always knew better than those around him. How did he manage to do that given that he did have an arrogant nature to him?

The answer is simple. Sherlock had taught himself *how* to control his behavior. Knowing his tendencies made it easier to apply the necessary changes, and thus get a hold of his impulses before they ruined the moment and gave his thoughts away.

Deep Breathing Exercises

Notice how when you're just about to explode with emotions, your breathing starts to race. This natural reaction is your body's way of coping with an increased blood pressure and heart rate, which both happen when you're brewing with heightened emotions.

Breathing deliberately, slowly, deeply, and from the stomach can help calm the nervous system and clear the mind. This can keep you from acting on impulse, allowing you to exercise greater control over your emotions, your thoughts, and your actions.

In many instances, Holmes would be described closing his eyes and breathing slowly and deliberately while he was being given information at a crime scene. This helped him keep his thoughts in check and prevent himself from saying anything that could interfere with the other person's behavior.

So, how can you perform deep breathing exercises properly to achieve the ideal socialization behavior? More importantly, how can you perform deep breathing in front of another person without giving yourself away?

1. **Unclench** - When confronted with another person who's talking or acting in a way that you might not find appealing or agreeable, the tendency is to clench the body.

Your shoulders might stiffen, you might feel your fists clenched tightly, and you might start to grind your teeth. These are all normal reactions when trying to control your impulses. But it can show outsiders that you're currently under stress.

Unclenching your body can help make deep breathing far more effective. This can be done by simply *letting go*. Start by sensing your face and detecting if your expression is tense. Relax your brows and try to keep your lips neutral. Then, move down to your shoulders. If they're raised and stiff, slowly let them go and drop them to their neutral position. Do this until you reach your feet, unclenching areas as you go along.

2. **Mindset** - Having the proper mentality can significantly improve the outcomes of deep breathing. For instance, if you refuse to let

go of negative thoughts or prejudices when you engage in deep breathing, then you might end up reinforcing these thoughts during the process. So instead of adapting the proper behavior, you would end up justifying and rationalizing your biases and tendencies.

With each full inhale, try to release your thoughts. The most difficult to deal with would be your own emotions, especially because most of us have been conditioned to operate on what we feel. Unfortunately, running on emotions can be very detrimental to social interactions.

As you exhale, let go of assumptions, biases, and ideas that could possibly interfere with the way you perceive or interact with other people.

3. **Breathe From the Stomach** - Deep breathing is actually synonymous with belly breathing - a unique breathing pattern that encourages you to inflate the abdomen instead of the chest. This form of breathing is particularly calming, known to help reduce heart rate and normalize blood pressure.

When trying to perform deep breathing, be sure to breathe into your abdomen. Take each breath slowly and try to feel the air as it fills your lungs. Hold each breath for around 3 seconds before completely releasing the air and inhaling again.

Empathize

We see the world through our own self-tinted glasses. What does that mean? It simply means that anything and everything around us is often interpreted according to how we think these different things might benefit or affect us. For instance, a teenage daughter being reprimanded by her mother for coming home late might think that her mother is being controlling and unreasonable, unable to see the reason why her parent might be acting that way.

Empathizing with someone - even if you've only just met - can help neutralize any feelings you might have. Take this scenario for example.

You're sitting in a cafe, enjoying a cup of coffee while you read your favorite book, and a woman comes barging in. She's shouting at the top of her lungs, looking for the owner of a vehicle she described to look just like your own. You slowly raise your hand and say that it sounds like she's talking about your car, and then she rushes to the side of your table and starts throwing minor insults your way.

How do you respond?

Considering that you've just met this woman, it's likely that you might find yourself wanting to engage in argument. *How dare she talk to me like this - it's mortifying!* Of course, the situation might cause a few heads to turn in your direction, but there are better ways to deal with this woman.

Firstly, you might want to take a few deep breaths. Before you address her, observe her behavior and her appearance. What could be her reason for acting this way? Would a normal person lash out at a stranger for no apparent reason? Probably not. What does she want you to do and what is she communicating to you?

As it turns out, your car was in the way of her vehicle, making it impossible for her to back up and drive away. She stopped by the coffee shop to pick up a drink for her boss who had no patience for late arrivals. This made her feel agitated, knowing how it might affect her work.

Putting everything into perspective, it's easy to see that while her reaction might not have been the best or the most appropriate, it definitely wasn't without reason. Learning to empathize with others in this way can help you control your emotions, especially when you come to realize that you might act similarly had you been put in a similar situation.

Add Context

Did you know that people are inclined to behave differently and put on a charade when faced with a potential employer? Did you know that people tend to wear different 'masks' depending on where they might be and who they might be communicating with?

We as a human race have evolved to *fake* interactions, especially when we feel that our typical behavior might not be ideal for a specific situation. Understanding this should help you become more receptive of other people and the way they might act around you.

We're often urged to adjust ourselves when the people around us don't act how we anticipate them to. *Why is this person avoiding eye contact? I should probably try to look more amicable. Why are they too close? I should square off my shoulders and lean away. Why do they seem aggressive? I should cross my arms and show them that I'm not intimidated.*

Don't. Remember that there is a context to every situation, and these people are probably showing you behavior based on *how* they think they should approach this particular interaction. Remain neutral and don't let them sway you into acting a certain kind of way.

Keep the Goal in Mind

One of the best ways to remember to keep your cool and to avoid tainting the interaction would be to keep your goal in mind. Your objective to decode and understand a person at a glance should be paramount to any emotional response that they might inspire.

In many cases, other people can make you feel upset or even angry simply by stating their own thoughts and opinions. Of course, it can be particularly difficult to resist the urge to fight back and respond how you would like to, but there are greater returns to taking the time to *understand* their behavior first.

By allowing yourself the cool, calm, collectedness that it takes to be able to properly decode a person first, you can stay one step ahead and react in the best possible way to avoid confrontation and arguments.

The Theory of Masks

An important aspect of understanding people at a glance involves understanding how each person has a tendency to use a mask. Even in their own personal space, a person might don a specific mask which makes it difficult to understand the true self.

Depending on the situation, it's possible that a person might use one of a variety of masks, allowing them to assume the most ideal self during a specific encounter. So how a person acts around family might be different from how they might act around coworkers.

Some people might develop masks to cover up specific traumas that they might have had in their earlier years. Those who suffered through abusive relationships as children have very intricate masks that make them exceptionally effective at deflecting any other people's efforts to get a glance into their truth.

These masks often work as defense mechanisms because humans are generally protective of their true self. Our objective during social interactions is to make sure that we're putting our best foot forward. No one wants other people to see the ugly realities of their actual selves, which is why it has become instinctual for us to wear masks to please the others around us.

What's tricky about masks is that they can be changed at a moment's notice. Most people can adapt and adjust their social mask in order to respond to slight cues in their given social engagement. For instance, a woman who feels that her date might think she's boring will adjust her posture and start talking about some of the more exciting events in her life, deflecting that train of thought and making him feel otherwise.

That said, it's important that you consider the theory of masks when trying to decode others around you. Using neutrality when dealing with a target will help keep them from adding layers to their mask, making it possible for you to see closer to the truth. The more encounters you have with someone, the less guarded they will become. So over time, that mask can change.

Honing Your Inner Holmes - DIY Experiment

Using the tips provided in this chapter and the previous one, try to respond to the following situations. Choose the answers that best suit your reactions in the options provided and see how well your choices match the ideal responses.

Scenario 1

A friend has set you up on a blind date with a someone who is a stranger to you. All you know about them is that they work at the local museum while completing their last few years of college.

You meet up at a local restaurant for dinner and they greet you with a timid handshake. After asking a few routine questions, the air turns silent and your date starts fiddling with their fork. They glance away and look at neighboring tables, giggling nervously as they point out something irrelevant in an attempt to clear the air of silence.

What do you do?

A. Prompt them with a question to start a conversation.

B. Let the air of awkwardness continue.

C. Ask them if they want to change the venue.

Scenario 2

At your work desk, you find a sticky note plastered across your computer screen. "See me IMMEDIATELY!" it says, scribbled in your boss' penmanship. You just got back from lunch and visited your desk to grab your toothbrush, so you dash quickly to the restroom and freshen up before seeing your superior.

You knock on his door and peer inside. You see him sitting at his desk with his hands on his head and his elbows resting on the table - a look of frustration drawn across his face. "What IS this?" he asks you. He's referring to a report that you submitted a few weeks ago.

The document was a summary of projections expected for the next few months of operations. The numbers weren't to his liking, but they were as accurate as you could manage. After all, the purpose of the report was to forecast the upcoming months, not to sugarcoat how things might happen.

He tells you to redo the entire report, which took you about a month to finalize. And on top of that, he requires that you render mandatory overtime so that you have time to work on the new output. Unfortunately for you, you've already made plans with your partner to spend time together since the past few months have been exceptionally busy for both of you.

How do you respond to your boss?

A. Apologize and say that you can't render mandatory overtime because you have prescheduled engagements.

B. Agree to his conditions and apologize for the way the initial report came out.

C. Offer to give an in-depth explanation of the report.

Answers

We all respond differently based on our own character and personality, but knowing how Sherlock does it should make it easier to react to social situations as ideally as possible.

Scenario 1

In the first scenario, your date is showing obvious signs of shyness. The routine questions, the aversion to eye contact, and the psychomotor activity in the form of fiddling with a fork are all classic signals that manifest a timid personality or uncertainty in that specific situation.

While it was explained that asking questions is an optional route when trying to decode a new person, you need to place this meeting in its context. A date requires more interaction, so it's important to make sure that you contribute to the engagement.

Given that, it's ideal that you add to the conversation *without* altering her behavior.

This means that you should try to avoid conversation starters that *suggest* that she share a specific pre-determined answer. This simply means that you should prompt her with a question (Option A) without giving her a hint as to what answer you're hoping to hear.

For instance, some questions are laced with hints that direct the individual towards an 'ideal' answer. "I'm a big supporter of animal welfare. How do you feel about animals?" With the initial statement, you've already told your date that you *like* animals, and of course, it would possibly be ideal for you that your date likes them, too.

Anyone in that situation would probably provide an answer that would impress the person asking, because the goal of a date would be to win the other person over. So even if they weren't particularly interested in animals, they might come up with some exaggeration of the truth or perhaps even a complete lie just to leave a good impression.

The best questions are open ended and non-suggestive, allowing the other individual to come up with an honest answer that could lead to further communication.

Scenario 2

In the second scenario, it's easy to see that your boss was upset about the numbers that came up in your report. Obviously, this wasn't the result of your mistakes, but the result of the actual data made available to you for the document. That said, it would be difficult to come to different results even if you repeated the entire process, given that you didn't commit any mistakes in the first.

Putting yourself in his shoes, it's apparent that his anger was possibly stemming from distress. The projections were less than ideal, and he was probably taking his anger out on the nearest possible target - you. Seeing things from his perspective, it's easier to see why he might be acting the way that he is.

It's always tricky dealing with a superior because of the power they have over us. In this case, your boss can have a direct impact on your job and career, so making the wrong move could result to detrimental outcomes for your work life.

In this case, the best option would be to explain your report (option C) to give your boss a better understanding of the numbers that appear in your document. Responding in a quiet, calm, and apologetic yet professional tone can help appease your boss and give you the opportunity to clarify the results of your calculations.

Chapter 4 - How to Interpret Personality Types

"London, noisy, noisome, nattering London: aged, ageless, dignified, eccentric in her ways - seat of empire, capital of all the world; that indomitable grey lady of drab aspect but sparkling personality - was at her very, very best and most radiant. And Holmes, ebullient and uncommonly chatty, was in a mood to match."

Let's hop back into the previous chapter and take a closer look at the second scenario in the DIY experiment. Given this reaction, what kind of personality do you think your boss had? Do you think he would have acted differently if he had a different personality? Yes, he probably would have. But *why* would a difference in personality have made a change in reaction?

An individual's 'personality' is loosely defined as a collection of traits and characteristics that give people their distinctive character. Throughout the years, there have been *countless* psychologists who have tried to encapsulate the meaning of a personality - from Freud, to Erikson, to Jung, and many others - and all of these experts have contributed greatly to our understanding of the abstract concept.

Essentially, our personality tells us what we think are the acceptable, ideal, and appropriate social reactions. Our inhibitions are dictated by our personalities, so there are some things that we may or may not do depending on our specific combination of unique characteristics. That's why some people find it easy to engage in arguments, while others find it more practical and reasonable to avoid confrontation even when they have all the reason to be upset.

Knowing an individual's personality is an important part of decoding people because it tells you *how* they might act or speak. Their personality will show you their tendencies and social patterns, allowing you to generate a more accurate prediction of how a specific encounter might go.

The Myers Briggs Test

Carl Jung was a Swiss psychiatrist and psychoanalyst who dedicated most of his life to understanding the human psyche. Through his research, he was able to publish several books that gave readers his interpretations and understanding of the human personality. Soon, English translations of these books found their way into the hands of Katharine Cook Briggs - an academic and an avid reader and writer.

Prior to finding Jung's books, Briggs had already developed her own theories on personality. She formulated 4 categories of personality types after noticing that her soon-to-be son-in-law had a different set of characteristics compared to members of their family. Upon reading Jung's books however, she discovered that the psychoanalyst had a far more extensive understanding of personality.

This prompted her to further develop her system, which led to the iconic Myers-Briggs Type Indicator - a personality test that she developed with her daughter, Isabel Briggs

Myers. This test is now used widely in employment and school evaluations.

Limitations of the Myers-Briggs Type Indicator

While it is widely used and applied in various fields of practice, the Myers-Briggs Type Indicator isn't without its flaws. In fact, throughout the years, countless critics have made comments about the MBTI's reliability, especially because it can give a person different results with each take.

On top of that, the test does not take neuroticism into account. So individuals with neurotic tendencies might not be detected by the exam. Finally, the test doesn't provide any accurate measures for what it detects, so it's hard to understand exactly *what* it tries to understand given that the concept of personality is so abstract.

Even then, using the Myers-Briggs for purposes

that include decoding a person can be good enough to get a better understanding of what lies underneath the surface. However, as any cautious detective, you need to be aware of the method's limitations to guide your premises and conclusions.

Concepts and Basics

The Myers-Briggs Type Indicator (or MBTI) is a personality test that can result to 1 of 16 different personalities. The test is administered by asking the examinee to indicate whether they agree or disagree to a statement by choosing an answer from a scale. This also measures the extent to which they agree or disagree.

Each personality type is defined by an acronym of 4 letters, each one corresponding to the specific inclination or tendency a person has which is determined to be *most prominent* in a list of dichotomies. There are 3 subcategories, and these are *attitudes, functions,* and *lifestyle preferences.*

Attitudes

The first letter in every Myers-Briggs personality type refers to either extroversion or introversion so that each of the 16 types will either appear EXXX or IXXX. This first letter designates the individual's attitude, which was described by Myers as the tendency to act either inwardly or outwardly on thoughts and ideas.

Essentially, extroverts are more inclined to *execute action.* They move and speak to fuel their motivation. Without this physical manifestation of energy, their motivation has a tendency to decline. People who are introverts are more likely to reflect and think. They prefer inward manifestations of their energy, and are more motivated with tasks that require rumination and deep thought.

Here are some of the basic differences of introverts and extroverts:

Extroverts	**Introverts**
Action oriented	Thought oriented
Prefer a wide knowledge base that crosses over to	Prefer a deep knowledge base that explains specific

different concepts	information in detail
Enjoy frequent interaction	Enjoy meaningful interaction
Draw energy from socialization	Draw energy from being alone

How do you identify an extrovert or introvert in public? Of course, drawing this information back to Sherlock, the true value of knowing the attitude types is being able to detect them in real life situations. In this case, you might consider someone an extrovert if they seem to enjoy socializing, if they seem energized with physical activity, and if they present a commanding aura that takes control of interactions.

You might call someone an introvert if they prefer isolation, if they enjoy small meaningful gatherings and socialization, or if they seem energized when given the opportunity to explore ideas, thoughts, and concepts away from the company of other people.

During social interactions, it's possible that someone who is an extrovert might be more interested in direct engagement and conversation. They also tend to be far more vocal about their ideas and opinions, making them quite the challenge to debate with. On the other hand, someone who is an introvert might be much more comfortable having you take the reins of a conversation.

Introverts, as a general rule, are far harder to decode because they internalize everything they think and feel. However, because they are more interested in *meaningful* interaction, tapping into what they find important and relevant can make it possible for you to get them to become more expressive.

Functions

There are two pairs of functions according to Myers - these are the perceiving and the judging functions. The **perceiving** functions describe how a person interprets information or data, and the **judging** functions indicate a person's tendencies when it comes to making a decision based on the facts that have been presented.

The <u>perceiving functions</u> are **sensation** and **intuition**. As a general rule, people have *dominant* traits in a specific dichotomy, but it never means that the other is completely disabled. Everyone has these traits to some extent, it's just that one or the other is more prominent and likely to be used.

Sensation pertains to a method of information processing that uses the 5 senses. This is a more empirical method of data interpretation in which a person prefers to rely on details that are perceivable. They prefer to dwell on data that's present, tangible, and *real* as opposed to information that comes from hunches or guesswork.

Intuition on the other hand, is a method of information processing that dwells more on the unseen. These people use their gut to feel for the right conclusion, even if that means their conclusion won't be based on factual, tangible information. They're often more interested in the possibilities of the future, so they won't limit themselves to choices that are bound by facts.

The <u>judging functions</u> are **thinking** and **feeling**. These are decision making functions that are used when a person needs to arrive at a resolve given a set of information.

As the term suggests, people who use their **thinking function** to make a decision choose to do so from a somewhat detached standpoint. They use logic and reason, and prefer to look at the facts before arriving at a thoroughly thought-out decision. However that decision affects their emotions or the emotions of others around them isn't a top concern in the decision making process.

On the other hand, people who use their **feeling function** when making a decision are more inclined to use the emotional context of the situation instead of simply dwelling on the facts. They prefer outcomes that generate harmony, making choices that suit the benefit and preference of the general census.

According to Jung, each person uses a dominant function in combination with an auxiliary function. The psychoanalyst has also suggested that we use a tertiary function to a much lesser extent, with the fourth function taking the role of a 'shadow'. In all cases, the shadow or fourth function is the opposite of the dominant function.

Lifestyle Preferences

In this dichotomy, there are two options - **judging** and **perception**. This is an added facet of the Myers-Briggs Type Indicator which wasn't available in Carl Jung's model. The purpose of this dichotomy is to decipher a person's preference in using either their judging or perceiving functions.

People who manifest the judging function as their lifestyle preference are those who navigate the world using their judging function most predominantly. This means that TJ individuals (or *thinking/judging*) are seen as logical people, while FJ individuals (or *feeling/judging*) are seen as empathetic.

In the same way, people who tend to prefer the perception navigate the world using one of the two perceiving functions. That said, individuals who are SP (*sensation/perceiving)* are seen as concrete individuals who use reliable facts.

Those who are NP (*intuitive/perceiving*) are usually considered or labeled abstract thinkers.

The 16 Personality Types

Although Jung had originally come up with 32 personality types, the Myers-Briggs Type Indicator condensed the types into just 16. These personality types use combinations in each dichotomy to come up with a holistic idea of a person's *tendencies*.

While it doesn't specifically predict a person's reactions, it does tell you the kind of response you can expect. The personality types shed light on the type of interaction a particular person might prefer, given the specifics they fall into under each dichotomy.

ISTJ	ISFJ	INFJ	INTJ
Sincere, analytical, reserved, realistic, hardworking,	Warm, considerate, gentle, thorough, pragmatic,	Idealistic, organized, compassionate, gentle, prefer harmony, enjoy	Original, innovative, independent, strategic, logical,

responsible, and trustworthy	devoted, caring, helpful, responsible	intellectual stimulation	reserved, insightful, driven
ISTP Action-oriented, enjoy understanding the mechanical functions of things, spontaneous, analytical	**ISFP** Gentle, sensitive, flexible, helpful, realistic, interested in practicality, strive for a personal space that's logical and beautiful	**INFP** Sensitive, creative, idealistic, caring, puts great value on inner harmony and peace, focuses on dreams and goals	**INTP** Logical, precise, reserved, flexible, original, enjoy speculation, can come up with creative solutions to problems, imaginative
ESTP Outgoing, realistic, action-oriented, curious, pragmatic, skilled negotiator	**ESFP** Playful, skilled at negotiating, strong common sense, friendly, spontaneous, tactful	**ENFP** Enthusiastic, creative, spontaneous, optimistic, supportive, enjoys engaging in new projects	**ENTP** Inventive, enthusiastic, versatile, inquisitive, strategic, enterprising, enjoys new and unfamiliar challenges
ESTJ Efficient, outgoing, analytical, realistic,	**ESFJ** Friendly, outgoing, reliable, practical,	**ENFJ** Caring, enthusiastic, idealistic, organized,	**ENTJ** Strategic, logical, efficient, outgoing,

systematic, dependable	helpful, prefer to please others, enjoys activity and productivity	diplomatic, responsible, skilled communicators	ambitious, long range planners, effective at organizing people

Understanding the personality types entails breaking its corresponding acronym down into parts. The first letter always represents the **attitude** which would either be extroverted or introverted.

The second and third letters are representative of the **functions**. As a general rule, this letter combination *can't* be represented by two letters from the same dichotomy. For instance, an individual can't be both *sensing* and *intuitive* since they're both perceiving functions. A person can't be both *thinking* and *feeling* since they're both judging functions. That said, the only combinations for the second and third letters can be **SF, ST, NF,** or **NT.**

Finally, the last letter in the 4 letter acronym represents the lifestyle preference for that specific personality. This can be either *perceiving* represented by P or *judging* represented by J.

All that considered, we can now decipher that a person who falls within the ISFJ personality type - the most common among the population - manifests an *introvert-sensing-feeling-judging* personality type.

Keep in mind that there's far more to each of these personality types than what's stated in this short table. In fact, each type comes with extensive elaborations that discuss the personality in depth, so it might be worth reading up on the different types to familiarize yourself with each one.

Stocking points of information for each type into your mind palace can help give you keys to understanding each person you encounter based on the type that you identify them to be.

Detecting Personality Types in Real Life

Is there any way that you can accurately determine a person's personality type based on the Myers-Briggs Type Indicator *without* putting them through the entire test process? The answer is **no**, you can't. Some of the factors in the Myers-Briggs personality types can only be determined by asking specific questions, so it might be impossible to get an accurate representation by strict observation.

On top of that, people have a tendency to wear a 'mask' depending on who they're in front of or where they are. Remember that according to Myers, just because a specific function is dominant, doesn't mean the others are disabled. For instance, a thinking person still has the capacity to feel, and a sensing person still has the capacity for intuition.

That said, some people will rely on less dominant functions if they feel that their current situation calls for it. For example, a person who doesn't like their job might use a secondary or even a tertiary function in order to finish the tasks at hand.

With that in mind, it's advisable that you avoid jumping to conclusions when trying to detect a person's personality type. Of course, Sherlock was able to decode personalities much faster, but we have to consider our own limitations as well as the possible 'masks' that people might wear to throw us off and improve their public image.

So, how can you accurately interpret an individual's personality type in the real world *without* putting them through the test? It's going to be tricky, but it is possible.

Are They Quick to Respond?

When interacting with someone, consider the speed at which they choose to answer questions. Do they respond almost instantaneously, providing long, drawn out answers that make it seem like they had these answers ready? Do they sound like they're thinking out loud, perhaps even dwelling into other topics from the actual answer to your question?

Or do they take their time before giving a response? Do they think about their answer before handing it over, and are their answers more limited and concise?

So, what's the relevance of being able to answer immediately or otherwise? Well, taking a closer look at this interaction behavior tells you whether a person is an introvert or an extrovert - the first letter in the personality acronym.

Generally speaking, extroverts are far more inclined to answer questions as if they're dictating what they're thinking because that's how they *think*. They function more efficiently in social interactions when they can voice out what they have to say, which substantially improves their train of thought. They NEED to think out loud because it's how they're able to come up with the best ideas.

On the other hand, introverts are the exact opposite. They prefer internalizing their thoughts, which is why they might take their time to ruminate before answering a question. They're less energized by social interaction and work best when they're left to their own devices, and it shows when you consider how they prefer to answer questions.

Conversations with introverts tend to be more laid back, logical, and slow paced, giving each contributor the opportunity to deliberate their answers and enjoy enough white space in order to craft a thorough response. On the other side of the spectrum, someone who's an extrovert might not give you the light of day.

These people *love* having the opportunity to talk which often takes over certain social graces. This means they might end up overpowering others involved, preventing them from sharing their own thoughts. In the event that two extroverts end up in conversation, then you might find them talking over each other in a conversational mess that almost sounds like unintelligible rambling.

Do They Like Talking About the Present or Past, or the Future?

You'll notice how some people seem to be far more interested in talking about things that have already happened or things that are currently happening, as opposed to things that *might* happen. These people obviously like to dwell on facts, and find it more reasonable to discuss things that are tangible and real.

In the same way, there are some people who prefer talking about things that could happen in the future. The thought of possibilities and the excitement of exploring what *might be* can be particularly interesting for these types of people, and they enjoy dwelling on ideas that aren't yet guaranteed or proven, but are likely to be true in the future.

If the person you're trying to decode is showcasing an interest in the tangible, or the things that have already happened, then they're likely to prefer their *sensing* function. If they prefer discussing the future possibilities, then they're likely inclined to use their *intuitive* function.

Do They Consider How Others are Affected?

People who use their *feeling* function are often more inclined to think about the way their decisions affect others around them. They're not always after the *best outcomes*, but are rather more interested in the *best solution for the people involved.*

On the other hand, the *thinking* individual makes decisions based on logical reason. How that choice affects others isn't exactly a major consideration when it comes to deciding on the best solution, as long as they arrive at the optimal outcomes given the specific problem.

Take this scenario for example: three families are on a road trip that's scheduled to run for about 8 hours. Each family will ride their own car, and the 2 cars will follow the head of the convoy to lead the way.

Two cars are both SUVs, capable of driving over rough terrain, which opens up the possibility of taking shortcuts that could reduce travel time to just 6 hours. This would be beneficial as it would prevent the risk of paying a late fee at the hotel, since they might arrive after the designated check-in hours if they travel the entire 8 hour stretch.

Unfortunately however, the third family is driving a sedan that can't tread through the dangerous, off-road terrain on the designated shortcut. So now, the families have to decide:

A. Two SUVs will travel through the shortcut and provide the sedan instructions on the long route in order to reach the hotel in time and avoid the late fee.

B. All three vehicles will travel the long route and just split the late fee among the three families when they arrive at their accommodations.

A *feeling* person would likely choose the second option because it *benefits everyone involved.* They would take everyone's emotional welfare into consideration, and use that to weigh heavily on an answer to a problem.

A *thinking* person would likely choose the first option because it comes up with the logical result. No one wants to pay a late fee, and given the proper directions, it's unlikely that the family in the sedan would be lost. Of course, that doesn't take the feelings of the third family into account, but the outcomes are optimal if they want to save money and time.

How can you determine if a person is *thinking* or *feeling?* Easy - asking questions about real life, world events can help showcase the logic they use to justify the decisions made by others around them. For instance, you can ask them about political events and then pay attention to find out whether they're inclined to choose what's *practical* or what's *empathetic.*

Are They Flexible or Rigid?

Imagine this scenario: Karen and Jonah are just about ready to have dinner. They had planned to cook up an elaborate meal to celebrate a recent promotion. However, since it has been a rather stressful day, Karen asks Jonah whether he'd like to have dinner out instead.

"Dinner out? But we already planned this dinner. Let's just reschedule your suggestion for tomorrow night." To which Karen responded, "Okay, do you want to try the new seafood place or do you want to make reservations at our usual?"

"The new seafood place sounds good," Jonah replies. The next day comes and just as night starts to fall, they're both getting ready to leave. "You know," Karen says, "there's this other restaurant we haven't tried. Marge told me they have the best tacos."

"We already decided on the new seafood place yesterday!" Jonah exclaims. "Let's not make any changes and just get our plan done."

Are you a Jonah or a Karen? If you consider yourself flexible and adaptable (like Karen), then you're likely a *perceiving* person. These people know that life isn't always as we plan, and so they revel in the ever changing flux of things around them. They're spontaneous and ready for everything, and they don't necessarily need plans to have a good time.

If you're more like Jonah, then that means you might be a *judging* person. These people like structure and certainty, and might feel thrown off if they don't get to follow their designated pattern of events. On the upside however, they are exceptionally talented at coming up with surefire plans and executing them, making them intelligent and efficient leaders.

Now What?

So, how do you use this understanding of personalities to be able to decode people at a glance? Remember that Myers specifically indicated that her Type Indicator wasn't a predictive measure to tell how people act or to measure their socialization preferences. Rather, it's an indicator of *tendencies*. Everyone has the *tendency* to act in more ways than one, but this Type Indicator allows us to see which tendency is dominant.

Understanding where a person falls under the 16 different personality types will shed light on their behavior and will thus give you a more reliable basis on which to establish how you should respond to them.

Honing Your Inner Holmes - DIY Experiment

Here's a fun test that you can try for yourself or that you might want to try on other people. These questions - although seemingly unrelated and irrelevant - are designed to give you a better idea of your own personality type. You can also use it to try to decode other peoples' personality types as well, according to the Myers-Briggs Type Indicator.

1. I like to...

    A. Meet new people and engage in social activities

    B. Stay at home and indulge in my favorite books and movies

2. I rely more on...

    A. Tangible facts and proven truths

B. Abstract thoughts and future possibilities

3. I base my decisions off of...

   A. Logic, reason, and rational thought to arrive at the best outcomes

   B. Empathy and the way the decision works for the general census

4. I prefer to...

   A. Have matters settled and be done with it

   B. Keep my options open for greater spontaneity

If you answered:

1. A - Extrovert

   B - Introvert

2. A - Sensing

   B - Intuition

3. A - Thinking

   B - Feeling

4. A - Judging

   B - Perceiving

Chapter 5 - Holmes' Super Power - The Art of Induction

"So what is the truth?" Mr. Umezaki had once asked him. "How do you arrive at it? How do you unravel the meaning of something that doesn't want to be known?"

- Mr. Umezaki, A Slight Trick of the Mind

Often, we mistake inductive reasoning for deductive reasoning because we hear the term *deductive* reasoning more commonly in the media! In fact, even Arthur Conan Doyle himself mistook one for the other, thinking that his character was a master of deduction when he was, in fact, a master of *induction*.

What makes them different?

To put it plainly, *deductive* reasoning is the process of logical reasoning that entails *taking* or *deducing* information from pre-established fact. Take this train of thought for example:

A. The authorities claim that this person was murdered. (FACT)

B. A bloodied knife is present in the room (OBSERVATION)

C. Thus, this bloodied knife must be the murder weapon (CONCLUSION)

It is *known* that the victim was murdered, and this becomes the basis for interpreting all the other information in the room. Thus, any observations made at the scene of the crime will be tied back to the initial fact.

On the other hand, consider this train of thought:

A. You walk into a room and find a dead body (OBSERVATION)

B. Near the body is a bloody knife (OBSERVATION)

C. There are stab wounds on the body (OBSERVATION)

D. The victim's hands are tied behind his back (OBSERVATION)

E. It would have been improbable for this person to stab himself given that his hands were bound (INFERENCE)

F. It's likely that someone else did this to this person (INFERENCE)

G. This person was murdered (CONCLUSION)

Upon entering this crime scene, you don't know any of the details. So any evidence that you collect at the scene will be treated as an observation. After collecting enough evidence, you can come up with inferences, or ideas as to how this information ties together. By considering the possibilities given the situation, you can then come up with a conclusion.

Often, Sherlock would wow the police and Watson with his superior inductive logic, which was often misbranded as deductive reasoning. The master detective had a knack for taking bits of information and details from each person he would encounter to be able to formulate a general idea or conclusion as to who they were, where they've been, what work they do, and many other extrapolations.

Using Inductive Reasoning to Decode Others

When Holmes and Watson first met, they knew close to nothing about each other, aside from the fact that they would now share lodging. Sherlock had to look for someone to split rent with him since he had been running short on funds. And that's how their paths crossed.

As they were introduced to one another, Sherlock said "You've been in Afghanistan, I perceive." He wasn't asking Watson for a confirmation, but was rather stating a fact. This surprised the good doctor. Sherlock didn't explain how he came to discover that bit of information until later on in the book, when John Watson tells him that he believes someone had told Sherlock of his recent trip to Afghanistan.

Sherlock explains no, that no one had told him and that he instead pieced together information based on what he saw and drew his conclusion from there.

Here's what Holmes' train of thought might

have looked like upon their first meeting:

A. Watson's face and hands are a darker tone from the skin under his cuff and collar.

B. This could mean that he was in a place that exposed him to harsh sunlight. Possibly a vacation?

C. If he were on vacation, then his entire body would have been tan.

D. He was not on vacation.

E. He was probably in a tropical country performing work-related activities under the sun.

F. Watson mentioned attending Bart's - a popular training ground for doctors.

G. Watson must be a doctor.

H. His stance is stiff and rigid, what someone might consider the typical stance of someone serving in the military.

I. John is likely an army doctor.

J. His arm is held in an awkward manner,

as though it causes him pain.

K. It might have been injured.

L. Considering all the premises, it can be concluded that John was an army doctor serving in a tropical country.

M. The Anglo-Afghan war concluded just last year. It was in Afghanistan.

N. John was an army doctor serving in Afghanistan, and was medically discharged after an injury.

Well, that was quite the mental exercise wasn't it? Sherlock had nothing more to go on than the things that Watson said during their first meeting, and the good doctor's general appearance. Piecing together all of this information without any pre-established facts, Holmes used his *inductive* reasoning to arrive at an accurate conclusion.

While it might take some getting used to, becoming adept at the use of inductive reasoning is very possible. Familiarizing yourself with the process and understanding the cornerstones of this unique type of logic can make it much easier to use it in real, practical situations.

Keep Your Eyes and Ears Sharp

Just like Sherlock, it's vital that you keep your senses sharp if you want to make the most of inductive logic. A lot of information can easily fly over your head if you're not paying attention, putting gaps in your premises and making it hard to piece things together.

Many of the little details you'll have to collect will be considered irrelevant and unnecessary by most, and at the start, you yourself might think that some information seems unimportant. But developing a keen eye that picks up on even the most minute details can help you collate enough information to come to the most accurate conclusion.

Observe as much of the person as possible, scan their body, grooming, their clothes, and mannerisms. Avoid putting labels or meanings on these readings unless you've weighed all the possibilities, and then decided on the most rational and realistic premise.

Leverage Online Tests

There are numerous websites that offer tests to measure and challenge your inductive reasoning skills. Tests are usually focused on finding patterns, and require you to find the missing or the next shape in a sequence.

These tests can be taken for free and are incredibly effective at sharpening your inductive reasoning skills. There are also a variety of other test formats that provide you situational questions, allowing you to flex your inductive reasoning muscle to piece the picture together.

Practice on Real People

Most of the people we see or come across during

the day will probably always be strangers to us, so there really won't be a way to verify if the conclusions you arrive at through inductive logic would be true or not. But it doesn't hurt to practice your skill when you can.

Taking the time to try to figure out more about the people you see in your day to day life can be particularly effective at helping you hone your inductive reasoning logic. This should train your eye to be far more sensitive when picking up minute details, and may even help you establish contexts for specific features that you would commonly observe.

Honing Your Inner Holmes - DIY Experiment

Here's a test to exercise your inductive reasoning. The next time you find yourself in a social interaction with a new person, try to use this short guide to help you learn more about them.

Keep in mind that while it is possible to use inductive reasoning to learn more about old friends, we tend to have biases when it comes to people we already know. So when sharpening your inductive logic, always try to find someone new.

- ☐ Observe the person's *fluid* traits. These are qualities that are not fixed and can be changed depending on preference or situation. (i.e. Hair, clothing, grooming, etc.)

- ☐ How are they kept? Are they well-maintained? Do you notice wear? Are they worn out and faded? Does it seem to be changed/cleaned/worn frequently?

- ☐ Based on what you've observed concerning fluid traits, what can you surmise regarding this individual's personality? Are they careful, meticulous, polished? Or do they seem carefree, free-spirited, and spontaneous? What other personality traits can you assume?

Observing the non-fluid features on your target

can shed light on a variety of details, some of which might not be as obvious to the typical observer. For instance, wear markings on a boot or a watch strap could indicate that that particular item is used frequently.

In some cases, it could also indicate routine. For instance, wear over an area of a watch strap could be because that person frequently fidgets with that part. The trick is trying to put context to the person's entire being by piecing together the different factors that they present. The more you're able to put together, the easier it becomes to put context into each specific detail.

Chapter 6 - The Body Scan Method

"Your problem, dear chap, as I have had occasion to remind you, is that you see but you do not observe; you hear but you do not listen. For a literary man, Watson - and note that I do not comment on the merit of your latest account of my little problems - for a man with the pretenses of being a writer, you are singularly unobservant. Honestly, sometimes I am close to despair."

- Sherlock Holmes, The Whitechapel Horrors

When Holmes told Watson that he perceived the doctor had come from Afghanistan, Watson's surprise was two-fold - one, because he knew for a fact that he hadn't told anyone that he had come from Afghanistan. And two, because he couldn't quite figure out how Sherlock would have figure it out. After all, they had just met.

Sherlock had a knack for keeping his methods concealed. So even as he scanned Watson's entire physique, the doctor had no clue that he was under such scrutiny. This was something that Holmes had perfected, successfully hiding any attempts he made at observation even from criminals themselves.

His thorough yet discreet body scan method was the ultimate weapon, giving him enough clues and information to draw inferences from and make sturdy conclusions about a person's character, behavior, and tendencies.

Executing a Quick Scan

The purpose of the body scan method is to collect as much information about a person as possible *without* giving yourself away. The last thing you would want is for someone to detect that you're trying to scrutinize them, which would likely urge them to become guarded.

That said, it's vital that you execute the strategy

in a tactful, strategic, and efficient way in order to get the most information without tipping the person off. In this light, it's appropriate that you understand the importance of using a system or pattern when executing a scan.

The Holistic View

The body scan starts off with a holistic view. During this step, you take in generalized factors of features that the person might manifest. This includes psychomotor activity, clothing, grooming, posture, movement, and verbal clues. There's a lot that you can decipher based on this information alone.

Psychomotor activity refers to what many of us might call *mannerisms*. A twitch of the eye, a need to twiddle the thumbs, nail biting, and tugging at the earlobes are all classic examples of psychomotor activity. So, why is it important to make a note of them?

As the name suggests, psychomotor activity is movement that might seem superficial at a glance, but is actually rooted in some psychological distress or disturbance. For instance, you might not find the need to bite your nails when you're watching TV, but when you've been called into your boss' office, then it might be a completely different story.

Often, these 'mannerisms' shed light on a person's current emotional state. Those that are closer to distress - like sadness, nervousness, fear, and anxiety - will all manifest some sort of psychomotor activity that the person might not be readily aware of.

Clothing can be trickier to assess because of the way that it might change depending on the situation. On top of that, we all have our own fashion and style preferences, so clothing choices tend to differ widely from person to person.

When scanning clothing, take into consideration the quality of the pieces (are they expensive, branded items?), the wear (do they seem like they're worn often?), style (is it revealing, conservative, traditional, outlandish?), and the cohesiveness of the outfit (do the items match?).

You can tell a lot about a person based on how well they're dressed. People who place particular emphasis on their image will likely throw everything else out the window to guarantee a polished appearance. Others who have limited time or resources might skimp out on clothing and settle for simply looking decent.

Posture has a lot to do with confidence, and is often the first thing people notice when seeing a new individual. A slouched, posture with arms pulled towards the sides or the center of the body showcases a shy, reserved, timid personality. These people might not be too comfortable being in social situations, and may feel guarded when meeting new people.

On the other hand, people who walk and stand with a straight back, who draw the hands away from the midline to assume a more open aura are considered more confident, not afraid to let other people in to see who they are.

Movements are also somehow connected to confidence, but they might also relate to how interested a person is in a specific topic. For instance, someone who particularly enjoys talking about world history might use exaggerated hand movements to bring a point across. Someone who might not be too interested in history might slump back in their chair and just let you do the talking.

A person who moves more readily and naturally is often seen to be more confident in themselves. Someone who chooses to assume a more stagnant countenance might be subconsciously trying to guard themselves to prevent other people from being able to penetrate through their personality.

Verbal clues exist not only in the content of what a person says, but in its delivery. A shaky voice amid nervous laughs and flustered speech could signal nervousness or surprise. Slow, deliberate talking littered with 'uhm' and 'uhh' could be indicative of an in-depth thought process happening behind the scenes.

Stammering is another verbal clue that you might want to consider. Some people, when fabricating a lie, might stammer between words out of nervousness. Fast talking could indicate a need for control and dominance as an individual attempts to get all their points across without giving any other person the opportunity to interject.

Face and Eyes

The face and eyes can give away a lot about a person. Many of the parts of our faces are designed to show emotions, which is why it's important to make sure you're paying attention to the right features when you're meeting someone and trying to decode them.

The **brows** are a great place to start, since these are often the most expressive parts of the face. Furrowed or a raised brow betrays internal thoughts of confusion, uncertainty, or skepticism. Gently raised brows with wide eyes can signal concern or mild surprise. Wide eyes and fully raised eyebrows can be indicative of shock.

Eyes that choose to look away even when being talked to might be guarded, nervous, or contemplative. In some cases, eyes that choose to disengage might also be keeping a secret, trying to prevent you from peering into their truth.

Side glancing can be a tricky thing to decode. In some cases, it might be as simple as recall since the eyes tend to 'search' the mind for information to be retrieved. In some cases, however, side glancing can be a sign of denial or disagreement, especially if the person doesn't seem to be pleased with what you're saying.

Arms and Hands

The arms and hands are another important aspect to make a note of. Hand movements will give you a clearer perspective of confidence and level of interest. But it's equally important to notice unintentional hand movements.

Mannerisms often manifest with the hands, and these little jitters are indicative of nervousness or other slight disturbances and distress. When people feel strong emotions but attempt to hide them, it's possible that they might manifest in the form of mannerisms, since the body needs an outlet to be able to relieve the overpowering feelings.

It's also worth noticing *where* the hands travel. For instance, a person who feels the need to keep stretching out kinks on a shirt might be particular about details, someone who keeps scratching or fiddling with their neck might be trying to soothe a wound. Some experts say that a person who keeps having to fix his or her hair during a conversation might be displaying romantic interest.

Legs and Feet

Finally, the legs and feet are the last important aspect of the body to make note of. The large muscles in these parts are often used to manifest excessive psychological distress that might be particularly pronounced. Significant nervousness often presents itself as a shaking leg.

The way the legs and feet are positioned also give away some information about a person's disposition. Feet that are spread slightly apart creates an open impression, which means that an individual is prepared and willing to take on conversation.

It's often normal for the feet to move and sway gently during a conversation, especially if you're seated. But take note of sudden changes in movement as they could indicate a point of interest during your conversation. For instance, a foot that suddenly points downwards as you shift topics might indicate excitement or disdain. You can confirm this by assessing how the person approaches the conversation after the switch.

Maintaining Discretion

The last thing you'd want would be to give yourself away during a body scan. Once the other person picks up on what you're trying to do, they may be prompted to act differently, covering up their true emotions and behaviors to make it hard for you to get a look inside.

Remember, people have a tendency to put on masks, and if they feel that their true self is being compromised, they can alter their mask to conceal what's real.

That said, your top priority should be to maintain the secrecy of your method to prevent your target from altering their behavior to throw you off. You can do this by following these steps:

Glide, Don't Fixate

It's easy to see when someone is *fixed* on a certain aspect of your being - whether it's your face, your clothes, your body, or anything else. So as a general rule, you should want to glide with your eyes instead of keeping them fixated on a specific feature.

If you notice something and want to inspect it more accurately, avoid looking at it for a prolonged period of time. Instead, glide your eyes away from your object of interest and return looking at it after a few moments have passed.

Leverage Body Movements

Your own movements can be used as a tool to help you inspect certain aspects of a person's being. Scratching your nose by tipping your head down gives you a moment of opportunity with your eyes away from your target's view. This can provide you the chance to look at other aspects of the person's being, from their legs to their feet.

Another technique that some people use is side glancing. Using your eyes to look away momentarily while you try to 'rack' through your brain for something to say - even if you know precisely what you want to express - can look exceptionally authentic especially if you know how to play your cards right.

Ask Directly

This tactic can be tricky to execute especially because it might tip your target off since it gives away what you're hoping to learn more about. But asking a direct question about something they *obviously* want to be noticed for brings an opportunity for you to inspect something else entirely.

A large piece of jewellery, a loudly printed shirt, newly colored hair, or a fresh pair of duds are all points of interest that can be brought up in conversation. As you ask about them, you might find your target fixated on the item of your inquiry, giving you a few moments to inspect other aspects.

Keep in mind that while it can be effective, asking too many questions about too many different points of interest can be considered odd, and may make your target feel guarded nonetheless. Asking one or two questions at most should give you the right opportunity without blowing your cover.

Chapter 7 - Your Survival Checklist - The Body Scan Method Condensed

"How long is this to last?" asked the inspector finally. "And what is it we are watching for?"

"I have no more notion than you how long it is to last," Holmes answered with some asperity. "If criminals would always schedule their movements like railway trains, it would certainly be more convenient for all of us."

- Sherlock Holmes, The Complete Sherlock Holmes

There is *a lot* to understand about the body scan method, and the meanings of these movements, mannerisms, behaviors, and qualities can change depending on the context they're presented in. On top of that, their interpretation can also change depending on the combinations of different factors that the person manifests.

What makes the body scan method hard to master is the fact that there can be a lot to pay attention to. For someone who isn't quite as experienced with the tactic, it can be a challenge to get everything down in one go, often leading to an unsystematic method that takes up too much time or even tips off the target.

To help you polish your body scan method, try to memorize this checklist to and store it away in your mind palace. The more you use this list, the easier it becomes to recall each item later on, making your body scan much faster and more efficient.

The Body Scan Checklist

General Body Behavior and Appearance

- ☐ Clothing

- ☐ Grooming

- ☐ Scent/odor

- ☐ Psychomotor activity

- ☐ Verbal clues

- ☐ Breathing patterns

- ☐ Demeanor

- ☐ Posture

- ☐ Movement

Face and Eyes

- ☐ Brow positioning

- ☐ Eye widening/squinting

- ☐ Eye movements

- ☐ Lip movements

- ☐ Lip biting

- ☐ Twitching

- ☐ Unnatural blinking

- ☐ Asymmetry

- ☐ Grinding of the teeth

Arms and Hands

- ☐ Openness (at the sides, crossed over the chest, toward the midline?)

- ☐ Movements (restricted, free, exaggerated?)

- ☐ Mannerisms

- ☐ Fixation (wounds, scars, rashes, clothing?)

- ☐ Grooming (nails)

- ☐ Shoulder height (relaxed, tense?)

- ☐ Skin (scratches, wounds, bruises, other marks?)

Legs and Feet

- ☐ Openness (facing forwards, slightly apart, facing sideward, kept together?)

- ☐ Movements (gentle swaying, rigid, sudden change in position?)

- ☐ Mannerisms (leg shaking, foot tapping?)

- ☐ Grooming

- ☐ Skin (scratches, wounds, bruises, other marks?)

Using and Building Your Checklist

Remember that the items on this list are intended to help you recall the parts of the body that you should pay attention to. These items aren't designed to help you *interpret* what to see, but instead serve as a guide so that you know where to look and in what order.

As you continue to use your checklist, you will start to notice other facets of a person's being that might be worth taking note of. Adding these items to your list as you go along will help you establish a more personalized checklist.

Once you establish a strong sense of your list, you can then start storing it away in your mental palace. Designating a special room for this entire list can make it easier to retrieve from memory. You might try using a model of yourself in your mind palace with labels on each part of the body that you might want to inspect.

Understanding What You See

What's the point of picking up on all these subtle mannerisms, movements, and behaviors if you can't possibly understand what they mean? Familiarizing yourself with the manifestations of internal feelings and thoughts can make it easier to understand what they mean when presented in a certain way.

Here are some emotions that you might encounter, and how they look when spoken through body language.

Anger

Anger is a strong emotion which is what makes it easier to detect than others. People who feel anger will manifest either direct eye contact without breaking it, or will completely avoid looking you in the eyes. If the latter is true, they might also roll their eyes and raise a brow.

Someone who feels anger might also bite hard,

making the jawlines more prominent. The face will assume a neutral, somewhat bored expression if the individual is attempting to suppress the emotion. In cases when anger might be overwhelming, the eyes are likely to widen and the nostrils may flare. When speaking, an angry person's voice might shake and become louder. The body may tense up and square off to face you completely. Psychomotor activity such as shaking the leg, or fidgeting with the hands may be present.

Disgust

A person who feels disgusted by something might wrinkle the nose and squint the eyes. In cases when they might want to suppress the expression, the eyes might widen slightly and the lips might twitch at one corner. The body - or a part of it - might tense temporarily. The fingers might stretch out as if in an attempt to avoid *touching* the idea of what is deemed disgusting.

Surprise

A sudden lock of the shoulders can signify significant surprise. Eyes may widen and the eyebrows are likely to fully raise. In some cases, the lips may part or may fully open. Some people also tend to use one hand to cover the mouth. Any psychomotor activity or mannerisms may cease temporarily as the person tries to process the unexpected information.

Fear

Fear comes in many forms, and the expression of this emotion can change depending on what causes it. In cases when a person might be trying to conceal the emotion, the lips may stretch horizontally and breathing may become rapid. Psychomotor activity may increase as anxiety starts to take over the system. You may also notice that the person will start to sweat, and they may start stuttering.

Happiness

As one of the most common emotions, it's easy for us to pick up on signs of happiness in a person's demeanor. Increased frequency of hand movements and gestures, widened eyes, smiling lips, and increased verbalization are all common signs of happiness. More subtle ways that happiness might show include slightly wider eyes, slightly raised brows, and increased psychomotor activity especially involving the legs.

Sadness

There's some stigma against sadness, and people are often convinced that it's something they should strive to hide. So sadness is typically suppressed, making it harder to decode compared to many other emotions.

Sadness has a tendency to cause an increased breathing rate, so people will try to normalize that by breathing deeper. This makes for a pronounced rising and falling of the chest as they put effort into trying to control the emotion. Sadness can also cause the corners of the lips to point slightly downwards.

A person might also choose to speak less as they try to regulate the feeling, so verbalizations might be reduced to single-word statements. Psychomotor activity may be completely absent or may be reduced to a gentle, rhythmic motion.

The spectrum of human emotion is definitely extensive, so there are far more to decode than just those enumerated in this list. That said, it's important that you continue to hone your skills and practice your technique in order to become more efficient at identifying the different emotions in the spectrum.

Similarly, you also need to be aware that feelings tend to overlap. Often, these emotions won't exist exclusively, so you need to figure out how they might manifest together.

The Purpose of Knowing

What's the importance of knowing how someone feels internally? Why do you need to pick up on emotions when trying to decode someone? The purpose of knowing is closely linked to the role that emotions play when it comes to behavior.

Revisiting the scenario of the angry boss, you'll notice that the way he felt played a pivotal role in his reaction to your report. Had he been less angry, then he might not have exploded the way that he did.

Knowing how a person *feels* will give you a better idea as to how they might behave in the present situation. This can help you tailor your approach so as to generate the most ideal interaction outcomes.

Conclusion

"A strange enigma is man."

- Sherlock Holmes, The Sign of Four

In our modern day and age, it can be exceptionally difficult to adapt Holmesian techniques because of the many different distractions and excesses that our culture teaches us to cling to. These factors have made it a challenge to decode people because of the mental clutter they create, making room for arguments, misunderstandings, and miscommunication.

While it's not a farfetched idea to think that perhaps Sherlock himself would have trouble understanding people in modern times, many of his skills are still relevant and effective tools to help reduce inefficient social interaction.

Whether it's for romance, for work, for family, or for friendships, there is a great benefit to knowing *how to read people*. This indispensable skill opens the doors to seamless communication and interaction, letting you get the best out of each encounter and mitigate possible disagreements.

We all want to live lives that have as little stress as possible, and learning how to decode the people around you can clear your social life of unwanted distress and difficulty.

So while you might not be able to use these skills exactly the same way Holmes did in his many exploits, they can still prove to be worthy additions to your mental toolbox to give you an edge and improve the way you go through everyday life.